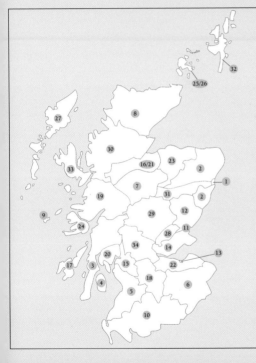

1. Aberd[...]
2. Aberd[...]
3. Argyll [...]   [...]ate
4. The Is[...]
5. Arran & Ayrshire
6. The Borders
7. The Cairngorms
8. Caithness & Sutherland
9. Coll & Tiree
10. Dumfries & Galloway
11. Dundee
12. Dundee & Angus
13. Edinburgh
14. Fife, Kinross & Clackmannan
15. Glasgow
16. Inverness
17. Islay, Jura, Colonsay & Oronsay

23. Moray-Speyside
24. Mull & Iona
25. Orkney
26. Orkney in Wartime
27. The Outer Hebrides
28. The City of Perth
29. Highland Perthshire
30. Ross & Cromarty
31. Royal Deeside
32. Shetland
33. The Isle of Skye
34. Stirling & The Trossachs

The remaining six books, *Caledonia*, *Distinguished Distilleries*,
Sacred Scotland, *Scotland's Mountains*, *Scotland's Wildlife* and
The West Highland Way feature locations in various parts of the
country, so are not included in the map list above.

PICTURING SCOTLAND

INVERNESS

COLIN NUTT
Author and photographer

2 The mouth of the River Ness viewed from Kessock Bridge.

INVERNESS

Welcome to Inverness! Fàilte gu Inbhir Nis!

Inverness (Inbhir Nis in Gaelic) has been known as the Capital of the Highlands for many years and was granted city status in 2000. It is a natural route centre due to its situation at the north-eastern end of the Great Glen and on the Moray Firth, which provided early settlers with a choice of secure elevated sites on which to live. One of these is the hill fort of Craig Phadraig, on the western side of Inverness. This is believed to be where St Columba met the Pictish King Brude, introducing him to Christianity in approximately 565AD. A later hilltop castle to the east of the city is said by some to be where Macbeth murdered King Duncan I in1040.

In more civilised vein, around 1150 King David I granted charters that gave Inverness Royal Burgh status. This privilege stimulated the development of the town, but in the troubled Middle Ages its growing importance made it a target for vying factions in the endless strife of that era. Inverness went through a cycle of prosperity and destruction (usually by being burnt), often as a result of royalty's attempts to bring unruly Highland clans into line. For example, Clan Donald burned the town at least seven times. The tensions between regional chiefs and the monarchy are also seen in Mary, Queen of Scots', visit to Inverness in 1562. Alexander Gordon, the castle's governor, refused her entry to the fortress which resulted in a siege. Once the castle was captured, Gordon was hanged.

4

Inverness from the air looking north-east, with the River Ness winding its way through the city. The expanse of sea at top right is the Moray Firth.

Fishing and shipbuilding were some of the early industries while the main exports through the port were wool, fur and hides. Later, brewing and whisky distilling developed. A foundry was established in 1872 and evidence of some of its work can still be seen in the suspension bridges that cross the River Ness in the city.

The River Ness defines the city, its name meaning 'mouth of the Ness'. The river is ever-present in the classic views of the city, many of which include the notable buildings on either side. It begins at the northern end of Loch Ness and for a short distance doubles as part of the Caledonian Canal. This famous waterway, built by Thomas Telford, opened in 1822. The last few miles of the canal diverge from the river and curve their way around the western side of Inverness, finally meeting the sea (in the form of the Beauly Firth) at Clachnaharry, a north-western suburb.

The first railway opened in 1855, initially from Inverness to Nairn. Eventually, connections went

6   St Andrew's Episcopal Cathedral with the River Ness in the foreground, seen from Inverness Castle

ight through to England, resulting in a ourism boom. Today's rail network still akes travellers over to the west coast at Kyle of Lochalsh, to the far north with ermini at Thurso and Wick and eastwards hrough to Aberdeen, as well as the main oute south to Edinburgh, Glasgow and England. This spectacular area, with its ugged mountains, deep lochs, rivers and rths, uninhabited wild places and notable owns and villages, provides a feast of ultural and visual treats for all who come o explore the region.

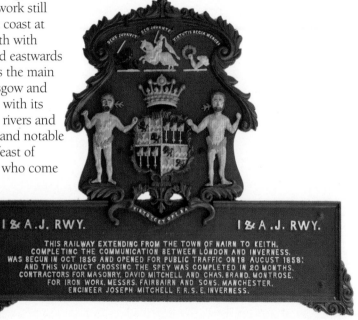

8   The mountains west of Inverness are barely noticeable in summer, but add a layer of snow and view through a long lens and the city's backdrop is transformed. The picture was taken from Alturlie on

he Moray Firth just east of Inverness. The mountain is Sgurr na Lapaich (1150m/3773ft) which is
bout 35 miles distant, so even in the clear winter air it has a slightly soft-focus look to it.

10 **Part 1 – along the Ness**. Inverness city centre as seen from Friars Bridge in December, with Christmas lights adding to the regular illumination.

Inverness has undergone major flood defence work in recent times which has changed the 11
architecture of the streets that line the river. Here, Huntly Street shows off its new look.

12 Looking across the River Ness from Greig Street footbridge towards Douglas Row, where attractive terraces of houses are now also fronted by the new anti-flood walls.

Left: also seen from the same bridge, the Old High Kirk is the oldest building in Inverness, part of **13** which dates back to the 14th century. Right: Free North Church framed in Greig Street Bridge.

14 Inverness Castle, built from 1833 to 1836. Today it serves various purposes including that of High Court for Highland Region. Plans are afoot to turn it into a major tourist attraction.

Close-up of Inverness Castle with a statue of Flora Macdonald, a heroine of the 1745-1746 Jacobite **15** uprising, on the right.

16 Looking north-west from Inverness Castle with Ben Wyvis in the far distance.

Left: again seen from the castle, a trio of church spires on Bank Street. Right: the *Three Graces* statue once stood on the roof of an Inverness department store but are now in a garden on Ness Bank.

18 St Andrew's Cathedral, situated by Ness Walk and built from 1866 to 1869.

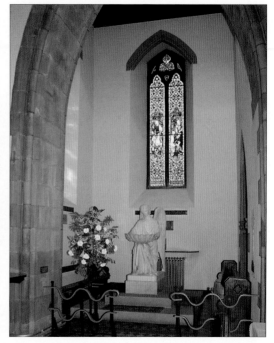

Interior of St Andrew's: the high altar, left, and the font, right. **19**

20 Inverness Castle floodlit at Christmas.

In 2018 Inverness Castle Viewpoint was opened to the public at one of the castle's highest turrets, **21** opening up a high-level vantage point up and down the river. This is the scene to the south.

22 It's the end of September and autumn tints are beginning to show in this view across the Ness, with the towers of St Andrew's Cathedral visible above the trees.

A little further up river, Cavell Gardens provide a lovely setting for the War Memorial on Ness Bank. **23**

24 The gardens are named after Edith Cavell, a British nurse during the First World War. She is
    celebrated for saving the lives of soldiers from both sides without distinction and in helping over

00 Allied soldiers escape from German-occupied Belgium. For this, she was shot by German firing squad.

26 The part of the gardens closest to the river has recently been improved and protected by sympathetically styled fencing.

Looking downstream towards St Andrew's Cathedral with Ord Hill behind. **27**

28 Eden Court Theatre on Bishop's Road is Inverness's principal performing arts venue. Its 830-seat auditorium runs a programme of plays, concerts and ballets. It also has a cinema and restaurant.

These decorative embellishments have been added to the grounds. The reflection of the theatre can **29** be made out in the stainless-steel spheres.

30 Bellfield Park, Island Bank Road, showing off its summer finery. Open air concerts take place at the park's bandstand during summer.

A view up-river from the castle towards Silver Pool footbridge, illustrating the Ness's sylvan **31** surroundings through much of the city.

32 Left: riverside villas at Lady's Walk on Ness Bank. Right: looking back across the river from in front of those same houses, a fly-fishing demonstration – this is a popular anglers' beat.

The Ness Islands add interest to the river upstream from here. A footpath winds its way through the **33** islands and across the river, allowing a circular walk.

34 Exotic blooms and some serious goldfish at Inverness Botanic Gardens. Formerly known as the Floral Hall and Gardens, they are an oasis of calm and beauty within walking distance of the city centre.

Part 2 – City Centre. Gerald Laing's statue in Falcon Square with detail of unicorn, right. **35**

36 The Alexander Dunbar Infirmary (almshouses), dated 1668, in Church Street. It was built from materials used in the Civil War citadel constructed in Inverness by order of Oliver Cromwell.

Left: Abertarff House, built 1593 and also in Church Street, is the oldest secular building in **37** Inverness. Right: Balnain House, built by a merchant in 1726, faces the river on Huntly Street.

38 Two imposing buildings on Bridge Street: left, the Town House, completed in 1882 and looking pristine following renovation. Right: the former Bank of Scotland building, now the Caledonian bar.

Interior of the Victorian Market and one of its more traditional shop fronts. The market lies within 39 the rectangle formed by Academy Street, Union Street, Church Street and Queensgate.

40 A classic Inverness panorama, from Young Street Bridge just visible on the left to tree-lined Ness Bank on the right.

42 Looking down Eastgate from St Stephen's Brae.

Inverness Museum and Art Gallery, with the Tolbooth Steeple of 1791 to its right. If it doesn't look **43** quite vertical, that's because it's not!

44 Part Three – outskirts of Inverness. By the shores of Loch Dochfour (the stretch of water between Loch Ness and the River Ness), rhododendrons in full flower make a fine sight in this loch-side estat

After utilising Loch Dochfour (left), the Caledonian Canal navigates its way through western **45**
Inverness. This stretch above Muirtown locks is busy with pleasure craft and boatyards.

46 Muirtown locks on the Caledonian Canal. The Canal opened in 1822 linking Inverness with Fort William at the other end of the Great Glen.

After passing through Inverness the Caledonian Canal reaches the sea at Clachnaharry **47** through one last lock.

48 Viewed here from North Kessock, the Kessock Bridge opened in 1982 and links Inverness with the Black Isle, carrying the A9 to the far north.

This is the opposite view, looking down from the Kessock Bridge to the village of North Kessock, **49** which was connected to Inverness by ferry until the bridge was built.

50 The Kessock Bridge is worth walking over to take in scenes like this. From the northern approaches this is the westerly view over the Beauly Firth.

Another fine view across the Beauly Firth is from the north side of Leachkin Brae to the west of 51
Inverness. Across the firth is the fertile Black Isle.

52 Just to the east of Inverness at Allanfearn, these ancient standing stones put their long-term perspective on the scene: having been here for millennia already, they will surely outlast the Kessock Bridge!

This picture makes an interesting comparison with the one on pages 8-9 – similar but different, **53**
another winter, another layer of snow, but different light and a different sky create a different mood.

54 Winters can last a long time in these parts: the foreground around the Moray Firth says it's spring, but Ben Wyvis is still covered with snow well into May.

The land around the Moray Firth is very fertile as this harvest scene testifies. The picture was taken **55** not far from the one opposite (near Alturlie), so the seasonal comparison is a point of interest.

56 **Part 4 – around Loch Ness**. Rainbow over Urquhart Castle. A legend relates that St Columba encountered the Loch Ness Monster here in the 6th century. One of Scotland's largest castles,

was reduced to ruins in 1692 to prevent the Jacobites from using it.

58 Fort Augustus is at the southern end of Loch Ness. Its focal point is the series of locks that lifts the Caledonian Canal towards the highest part of its route.

The canal remains a busy waterway. On this occasion a group of beautifully preserved vintage boats **59** is passing through, heading south towards Fort William.

60 The southern shore of Loch Ness near Fort Augustus, from where it stretches 23 miles/37 kilometres north-west towards Inverness. In places it is over 230m/750ft deep. Sadly, no monster on this occasion

The hills around Loch Ness hide many other smaller lochs, in exquisite settings. This is Loch Tarff, **61** tucked away in the hills on the southern side of Loch Ness, not far from Fort Augustus.

62 Now we return to the north side of Loch Ness, where Urquhart Castle is imposingly situated with commanding views to north and south. Its origins as a fortress possibly go back to the Iron Age.

From Urquhart Castle it is only a short distance on to the village of Drumnadrochit, where this floral **63** version of the castle is a point of interest on the village green.

64 Left: the Falls of Foyers, in the village of the same name on the south side of Loch Ness, form a spectacular sight with a drop of 49m/160ft. Right: the ravine of Foyers Glen drops steeply to Loch Nes

The Great Glen experiences temperature inversions quite often, mostly in spring or autumn, resulting **65** in thick mists like this. Meall Fuar-Mhonaidh (on the right) appears to be floating on the clouds.

66 The classic viewpoint for Loch Ness sunsets is at the village of Dores at the northern end of the loch, by the Dores Inn. Loch Ness contains more water than all the lakes in England and Wales put together

Taken about an hour later, this picture shows how the 'light show' can go on after the sun has set
as the cloud patterns change.

68 Not far from Dores, up in the little-known district around Dunlichity, a pattern of lochs invites exploration. Here we see Loch Duntelchaig early on an autumn morning.

Close by is the smaller Loch a' Clachan, an absolute gem in its setting of craggy hills. **69**

70 **Part 5 – Glen Affric**. Now we go north of the Great Glen to the mountains around Glen Affric. On the way, our route passes the reservoir Loch Beinn a Mheadhoin, which has created its own fine landscape

Located about 30 miles south-west of Inverness, Glen Affric is famed as being one of the most **71** beautiful glens in Scotland. This late-winter scene shows its moodier side.

72 In summer when Loch Affric is blue and the heather is in full bloom, a very different impression is
created. The mountain on the right is named Sgurr na Lapaich (meaning peak of the bog), but it's

ot the one we've seen earlier in this book. However, it does form part of the route we'll be taking in n exploration of the Glen Affric mountains.

74 Our route begins in Glen nam Fiadh, the next valley to the north of Glen Affric, where this waterfall makes an ideal foreground to the mountains beyond.

Further up Glen nam Fiadh the summits on this walk come into sight, with Tom a' Choinich **75** (1112m/3648ft) in the middle distance and Mam Sodhail (1181m/3875ft) in the far distance.

76 Up on the undulating ridge between Tom a' Choinich and Carn Eighe, vertical rock strata have eroded into some needle-like forms. Glen Cannich (see pages 78-79) lies beyond.

The far point of this walk is Carn Eighe which, at 1183m/3881ft, is the highest point north of the
Great Glen. This is the southerly view with Ben Nevis in the centre distance, about 30 miles away.

78 The next valley north again is Glen Cannich. In this winter-wonderland scene, the snow in the foreground has turned into ice crystals, giving it an amazingly sparkly appearance.

Glen Cannich's reservoir, Loch Mullardoch, lies frozen on its shadier side. This is a glen that is **79** missed by many, but its solitude adds to the enchantment for those who do come here.

80 **Part 6 – trips from Inverness**. The attractive town of Beauly is situated about 12 miles west of Inverness. The town square, seen here, is where a number of interesting features are located.

Beauly's origins go back to the founding of the Priory in 1230 by the Valliscaulian order, **81** one of three they established in Scotland.

82 The interior of Beauly Priory's church, the only remnant of what was once a monastery, complete with all the usual affiliated buildings. Around 1510 the priory changed its adherence to the Cistercian order

Left: an immense oak tree in Beauly Priory churchyard must have witnessed centuries **83** of the village's history. Right: Boer War Memorial in The Square, Beauly.

84 The Moray Firth is home to a great variety of marine life including Grey Seals . . .

. . and Bottlenose dolphins. Where they might appear is, of course, unpredictable; however the narrow **85** stretch of the Firth between Fort George (see pp.98-103) and Chanonry Point is a good prospect.

86 An aerial view of Tomatin Distillery, near the village of the same name, about 15 miles south of Inverness. Distillery tours are available. Follow the railway line on the left north a few miles and . . .

. . . come to Culloden viaduct, through the arches of which the early morning sun filters and casts **87** shadows on the fields, as the morning train from Inverness to London gets into its stride.

88 From the hill fort of Craig Phadraig on the western outskirts of Inverness, this scene stretches away to the west along the Beauly Firth and to the hills beyond. The town of Beauly lies just beyond the

...och shore at the top right of the picture.

90 Culloden Battlefield on the moors just east of Inverness is one of Scotland's most important historical sites. It is the location of the last battle fought on British soil.

A piper and 'soldier' at the annual service of remembrance at the commemorative cairn on the **91** battlefield. The one-sided battle of 16th April 1746 finally and brutally ended the Jacobite uprisings.

92 Leanach Cottage survived the battle and remained in use for over a century-and-a-half. Its last inhabitant, a Mrs MacDonald, left in 1912.

Some of the many grave markers at Culloden. The new visitor centre does an excellent job of **93** explaining and interpreting the battle and its causes – do go there to discover the full story.

94 Ancient remains are plentiful around Inverness: here, east of the city in the valley of the River Nairn are Clava Cairns, an extensive collection of Bronze Age standing stones and chambered cairns.

Looking out from the inside of one of the Clava Cairns.

96 Left: an aerial view of Cawdor Castle, situated a few miles east of Culloden.
Right: the Drawing Room of Cawdor Castle.

Cawdor Castle dates from the late 14th century and was built as a private fortress by the Thanes of Cawdor. It is open to the public from May to early October.

98 Fort George, on the Moray Firth near the village of Ardersier, was built to discourage further uprisings after Culloden. Pictured are the drawbridge and a rotating gun emplacement.

Fort George is one of the most outstanding fortifications in Europe, taking 21 years to build from **99** 1748 to 1769. This view shows the Guardroom block. Inset: a Spitfire flies over the fort.

100 Fort George holds a number of historical re-enactment events each year. Here, a skirmish from the 17th-century Covenanter War is recreated with loud musket fire adding realism.

Also at Fort George, but on a lighter note, these dancers show off their moves from **101** a Second World War-era dance floor complete with Swing band.

102 The Second World War area of one of the re-enactment days, with some of the accommodation blocks beyond – Fort George remains an active Army barracks.

Left: a look-out post at Fort George. Right: The final stop on this journey is the seaside town of **103**
Nairn where this beautifully crafted Fishwife statue stands on the seafront.

104 This winter landscape was captured from Tomhommie, a hamlet between Ardersier and Nairn. The mountain in the background is Ben Wyvis (1045m/3428ft), about 25 miles away.

106 Nairn has an excellent and extensive beach. Perhaps it is no surprise that Nairn was once branded as the 'Bournemouth of the North'. It is still an excellent place for a seaside holiday.

Nairn Museum specialises in local history, with artefacts and collections of local life, including this reconstruction of a home from an earlier era. Well worth a visit!

108 Nairn's War Memorial and surrounding garden, located on Cawdor Road.

The annual Nairn Highland Games are held on The Links. Here, a caber is in mid-toss, **109**
under the watchful eyes of the adjudicators.

110 Nairn harbour in winter. Like Inverness, Nairn benefits from the Moray Firth micro-climate.

Top: early morning in summer at Nairn Links, complete with bandstand. Below: a last look at Nairn **111** beach, with mountains miles away in Wester Ross for a backdrop – but that's another journey. . .

Published 2019 by Lyrical Scotland, an imprint of Lomond Books Ltd, Broxburn, EH52 5NF
www.lyricalscotland.com www.lomondbooks.com

Originated by Ness Publishing, 47 Academy Street, Elgin, Moray, IV30 1LR
(First published 2008 by Ness Publishing, 2nd edition 2011, reprinted 2014, 3rd edition 2016)

Printed in China

All photographs © Colin and Eithne Nutt except pp.5 & 86 © Scotavia Images; pp.84 & 85 © Charlie Phillips;
pp.96 (both) & 97 © Cawdor Castle; p.107 reproduced by permission of Nairn Museum

Text © Colin Nutt
ISBN 978-1-78818-077-1

Front cover: the River Ness and Inverness Castle; p.1: an Inverness cameo; p.4: close-up of Flora MacDonald statue
at Inverness Castle; this page: close-up of the fine detailing on Nairn bandstand; back cover: sunset over Loch Ness